EVOLUTION

CW00734920

eXtreme Facts

BY STEFFI CAVELL-CLARKE

©2019
The Secret Book
Company
King's Lynn
Norfolk PE30 4LS

Written by:
Steffi Cavell-Clarke
Edited by:
Holly Duhig
Designed by:
Danielle Rippengill

ISBN: 978-1-912502-35-6

All rights reserved
Printed in Malaysia

A catalogue record for this book
is available from the British Library.

All facts, statistics, web addresses and URLs in this book were verified as valid and accurate at time of writing.
No responsibility for any changes to external websites or references can be accepted by either the author or publisher.

PHOTO CREDITS

Abbreviations: l-left, r-right, b-bottom, t-top, c-centre, m-middle.

4mr – Vlad_Nikon, 4bl – K.Narloch–Liberra, 4br – Mr. SUTTIPON YAKHAM. 5tl – Monthira, 5mr – Darren Whittingham, 5ml – CHAINFOTO24, 5br – Vlad_Nikon. 6b – DLA. 7tr – donfiore, 7b – Elena Krivorotova. 9tr – Mr. SUTTIPON YAKHAM, 9bl – Annotee. 11tl – Monthira, 11bl – Krievenko Photo, 11br – Vadim Fedotov. 13tl – CHAINFOTO24, 13tr – Simon Tang, 13br – CHAINFOTO24. 15tl – Monthira, 15bl – Vlad_Nikon, 15br – Vlad_Nikon. . 17tl – aodaodaodaod, 17mr – Ekkaluck Sangkla, 17bl – Fogey. 18bl – Kevin Bluer, 18br – I WALL. 19tl – John99, 19ml – MylImages – Micha, 19br – K.Narloch-Liberra. 20m – holbox. 21tl – Darren Whittingham. 23tl – Eric Isselee, 23m – Rich Carey, 23bl – pim pic, 23bm – Nomad_Soul, 23br – Jon Nightingale.

Images are courtesy of Shutterstock.com. With thanks to Getty Images, Thinkstock Photo and iStockphoto.

CONTENTS

Words that look like this can be found in the glossary on page 24.

THE EVOLUTION OF LIFE

Evolution explains how life on Earth has developed over _billions_ of years. Life on planet Earth started as single type of _microorganism_, but has developed to include thousands of _species_ of bird, insects, fish, reptiles and mammals.

4.5 billion years ago Earth was formed

530 million years ago **first fish** appeared

3.8 billion years ago first microorganisms appeared

475 million years ago first land plants **appeared**

370 million years ago first amphibians appeared

4

150 million years ago first birds appeared

65 million years ago dinosaurs became extinct

200 million years ago mammals appeared

2.5 million years ago the first human species appeared

225 million years ago dinosaurs appeared

200 thousand years ago modern humans, called Homo sapiens, first appeared

320 million years ago first reptiles appeared

Evolution never stops, it is happening around us all the time.

5

PLANET EARTH

Most scientists agree that planet Earth was formed around 4.5 billion years ago.

When it was first formed, **Earth was a ball of red-hot,** liquid rock and could not support life.

Over billions of years, the temperature on Earth began to cool and water appeared on the **surface of the planet.**

Earth has not always looked the way it does today. Over millions of years, planet Earth changed. The land moved and shook and volcanoes erupted.

Water is needed to create life on planet Earth. All living things need water to survive.

Once there were oceans, tiny microorganisms began to grow and life began!

Planet Earth has an <u>atmosphere</u> full of <u>gases</u>, but over millions of years it was filled with lots of oxygen, which humans and animals need in order to breathe.

Atmosphere

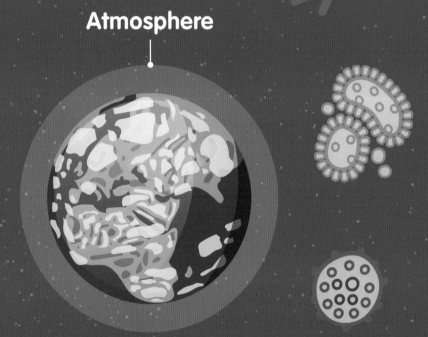

475 million years ago, plants began to grow on the land, which tempted the creatures out of the sea and onto the Earth's surface.

NEW LIFE

Life first appeared on Earth around 3.8 billion years ago.

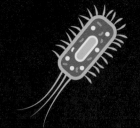

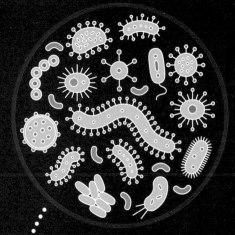

The very first life forms were single-cell microorganisms called bacteria. Microorganisms are so small that they can only be seen through a microscope.

Over billions of years, the early microorganisms developed to form bigger and more complex living things, such as plants.

Microscope

The first animals **living on the land were** plant-eaters.

Some fish adapted to live on land, and evolved into the first <u>amphibians</u>.

The very first reptiles developed from amphibians who laid their eggs on land.

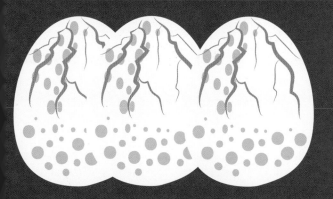

The first mammals **evolved about 220 million** years ago and developed into many different species, including **humans.**

DINOSAURS

Dinosaurs evolved about 225 million years ago from a group of reptiles.

Dinosaurs walked the Earth for over **165 million** years.

The word dinosaur means 'terrifying lizard'.

There were many small dinosaurs, but there were some giant ones too!

Scientists think that one of the largest **dinosaurs weighed around 50 tonnes.** That's around the same as 50 polar bears.

Scientists believe that some dinosaurs developed feathers and the ability to fly.

Not all dinosaurs were meat-eating **predators.**

The **barosaurus** was a giant, long-necked dinosaur that only ate plants.

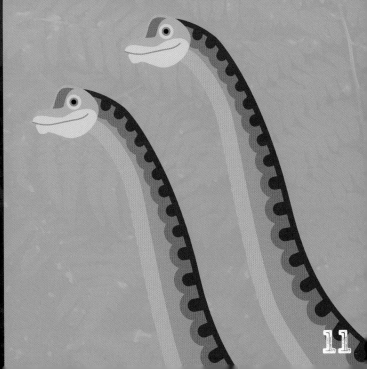

Some scientists believe that dinosaurs became extinct due to extreme changes in the <u>climate</u>, or because of a huge meteorite hitting the Earth.

FOSSILS

Fossils are the remains of plants and animals that have been <u>preserved</u> in rocks.

Scientists use fossils to work out Earth's history and the history of life.

Without fossils, we wouldn't even know that dinosaurs once walked the Earth.

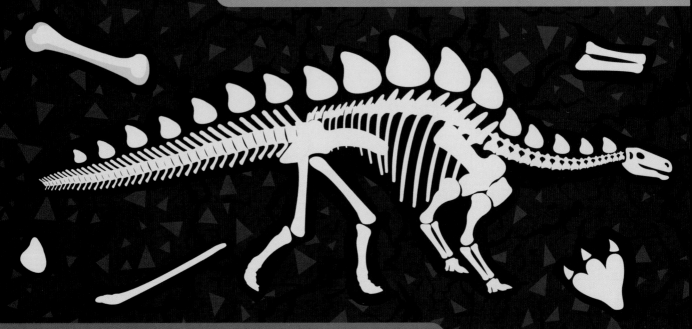

Some fossils can form in just 10,000 years, but most take much longer.

Fossils can show us the living things that existed millions of years ago.

Fossils can also show us things like footprints, egg shells and nests.

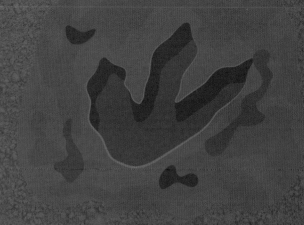

Even poo can be **fossilised!**

A fossilised poo is called a **coprolite**. A coprolite can tell us a lot about an animal's life.

Fossils help us to understand the history of life on Earth because they show us how animals have changed and adapted over time.

CHARLES DARWIN

In 1831, a <u>naturalist</u> called Charles Darwin set out on a five-year-long journey to learn more about the natural world.

He sailed on a ship called the HMS Beagle and travelled across the globe.

On his journey, Darwin visited the Galápagos Islands.

He discovered animals that only lived on those islands, such as giant tortoises.

On the Galápagos Islands, Charles Darwin found a species of bird called the finch. The finches had differently shaped beaks depending on which island they lived on.

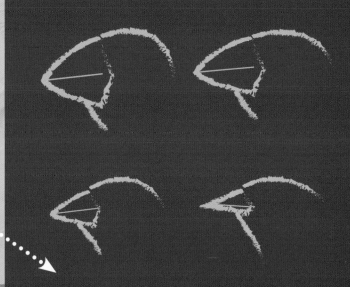

He noticed the beaks were **adapted** to eat the different food sources on each of the islands.

Darwin realised that the same species could change or adapt over a long period of time.

This change could be so great that a whole different species could be created. This is the process of evolution.

Lots of people disagreed with Darwin because they believed that God created all living things. But Darwin believed that different species of animal were created through evolution.

NATURAL SELECTION

Within any species of animal, there will be some <u>variations</u> in their <u>characteristics</u>.

Some variations make an animal's life easier, whereas other variations can make an animal's life harder.

Charles Darwin had the idea that animals who are better suited to their environment survive and pass on their <u>traits</u> to their offspring. Animals who are not will slowly die out.

Let's take a closer look!

Some beetles in this same species are brown and others are green.

Green beetles are **easier** for birds to see.

This means that they are **more likely** to be eaten, therefore, they are **less likely** to produce offspring.

The brown beetles have more chance to have offspring because they have a better chance of survival, which means that the number of brown beetles will go up.

Eventually, **every member** in the beetle species will be **brown**. The species will have adapted over time to its environment.

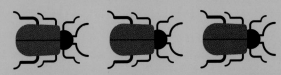

ADAPTATION

Living things have survived through freezing <u>ice ages</u> and blistering heat waves. They did this by adapting.

Adaptation means that, over a long period of time, species can change their traits to survive in different environments.

The animals and plants that have adapted to suit their environments are much more likely to survive than those that haven't.

Adaptations occur in every species.

Turtles have adapted to swim underwater **for hours without coming up for air.**

Polar bears have adapted to have a heavy coat of fur and a thick layer of fat to help keep them warm.

Giraffes have adapted to have longer necks so they can eat leaves on higher trees.

Flatfish have adapted to change their skin colour to match their surroundings to avoid being eaten by predators.

MONKEY TO MAN

Human evolution is a very long process. Our ancestors would have looked very different to how we look now.

Scientists agree that our early ancestors, Homo erectus, first appeared in Africa around two million years ago.

Homo erectus means 'upright human' and it was given to Homo erectus because they stood upright on two legs.

Over time, these humans evolved into Homo sapiens; the humans that we are now!

It is thought that humans and apes share a common **ancestor.**

This means that, although we did not evolve from apes, we are distantly related to them.

Homo sapiens have complex brains that have helped us to develop languages to talk to each other and use tools to build and make things.

The entire process of human evolution has taken around **6,000,000 years.**

EXTINCTION

A species of animal is said to be extinct when every individual in that species is dead.

When a species becomes extinct, the evolutionary process ends.

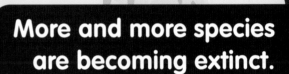

More and more species are becoming extinct.

Scientists estimate that between 150 and 200 different species of animal, plant and bacteria become extinct every day.

Lots of things can cause a species to become extinct.

Pollution is the biggest threat to living things on our planet. Pollution harms animal habitats too.

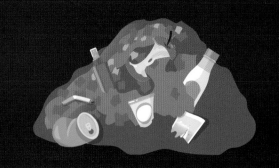

Humans pollute the planet in many different ways, but you can help stop pollution today.

Here are three easy ways that you can help to stop pollution:

Recycle your rubbish

Remember to turn off lights and computers

Reuse plastic shopping bags

GLOSSARY

amphibians	animals that live on both land and in water
ancestors	persons from whom one is descended, for example a great-grandparent
atmosphere	the mixture of gases that make up the air and surround the Earth
billion	a thousand million
characteristics	features of something that help to identify it
endangered	when a species of animal is in danger of going extinct
gases	air-like substances that expand freely to fill any space available
ice ages	periods of time in the past when the Earth was very cold.
microorganism	a single cell that can only be seen through a microscope
naturalist	an expert in natural history
offspring	an animal's young
oxygen	a natural gas that all living things need in order to survive
predators	animals that hunt other animals for food
preserved	maintained in its original or current state
species	a group of very similar animals or plants that are capable of producing young together
traits	qualities or characteristics of a living thing
variations	a different form of something else

INDEX